Hinge

Crab Orchard Series in Poetry
OPEN COMPETITION AWARD

HINGE

Molly Spencer

Crab Orchard Review
& Southern Illinois University Press
Carbondale

Southern Illinois University Press
www.siupress.com

23 22 21 20   4 3 2 1

Cover illustration: Doorknob in the shape of a human hand, close-up;
   Johner Images via Getty Images

The Crab Orchard Series in Poetry is a joint publishing venture of
   Southern Illinois University Press and *Crab Orchard Review*. This
   series has been made possible by the generous support of the Office
   of the President of Southern Illinois University and the Office of
   the Vice Chancellor for Academic Affairs and Provost at Southern
   Illinois University Carbondale.

Editor of the Crab Orchard Series in Poetry: Jon Tribble
Judge for the 2019 Open Competition Award: Allison Joseph

Library of Congress Cataloging-in-Publication Data
Names: Spencer, Molly, author.
Title: Hinge / Molly Spencer.
Description: Carbondale : Crab Orchard Review & Southern Illinois
   University Press, 2020. | Series: Crab Orchard Series in Poetry
Identifiers: LCCN 2020004615 (print) | LCCN 2020004616 (ebook) |
   ISBN 9780809337972 (paperback) | ISBN 9780809337989 (ebook)
Classification: LCC PS3619.P4658 H56 2020 (print) |
   LCC PS3619.P4658 (ebook) | DDC 811/.6—dc23
LC record available at https://lccn.loc.gov/2020004615
LC ebook record available at https://lccn.loc.gov/2020004616

Printed on recycled paper ♻

This book is for my family—every single one of you.
And for Mary.

Water, is taught by thirst.
Land — by Oceans passed.
Transport — by throe —
Peace — by its battles told —
Love, by Memorial Mold —
Birds, by the Snow.

> —*Emily Dickinson*

Contents

Hinge

I

SELF-PORTRAIT AS THE RIVER FLOODS

Snow chokes this town like a plague.
Slumped walls of white,
every corner clotted. March
comes in dazed—the sun
a weak rumor, quivering
hills, a just-begun dream
of runoff. I go back
years to the town of high ground,
that first yard necklaced by creek
and stone, berries brambling
down the backyard hill.
I go back—crocus
striving through snow,
all the orchards waiting
to blush then break
open. Now I know
not to sink too deep in the folds
of the bed, that even floors
can wander. Nights
of crest and sandbag,
the borrowed bridge
to safe ground swamped
by morning. I go down
to watch the water's surge
and spoils—there goes our table,
there, the spare key, there go
the stories I told them.
The children are growing
long and ravenous.
What can I build
that will hold?

ONSET

Late snow, and after,
the orchard tamed, unblossomed.
That waking

to a stunted world,
the clock made loud
and slow.

Say your mother found you
hot and aching, wooden, warped, your bones
made sudden by pain.

Say she said, Rest, and you rested,
hearing far voices—the bodies
you'd birthed—down hallways long and bare.

Say she said, Take this, and you took it.
Then slept. A sheet pulled tight,
the whole world whitening. Sooner or later,

every house has a sick room—
pale walls built by weather and waiting.
A window for weak light, the door forever ajar.

Sooner or later, every orchard
knows the slow burn—bales of wet hay lit
in rows, smoldering in a cold snap. Weak heat

and too late. A bleak
unharvesting, the coming summer
fruit-shorn.

Once there was no body,
just the strange spell of self.
A hand told to hold would hold.

Once a woman learned the weight
of flesh and bone, an earthward pull,
that fisted shape—a blossom held in snow.

DEMETER, SEARCHING

Days I hunted the mend
where earth had torn. Dowsed
with my forked heart for her slow river of tears.

Went home, looked under the bed.
In the stalled closet, leafed through her sleeves
for clues. Even laid myself down

on the thatched field, listening
for the deep *thud-thud*
of his headboard against the wall.

Counted months by moon phase,
left the stove and washing, turned
the garden graveward, stacked wood.

Until there she was in my kitchen,
taller than before,
a basket of wash on her hip.

It was hours of scrubbing and rinsing, hours
of pinning bleached petals of slip
and lament on the line before I asked,

Where? It was hours
before her deep-water reply: Mom,
Mom. It's not the kind of place you can point to.

SURVIVAL GUIDE FOR THE GIRL TRYING TO AVOID CAPTURE

This is the season of earth drain, of all that's bare
and pleading. Wear gray. You will blend

in with the deer who are also quiet.
Be mute. When they question you, only gesture.

Of course this means you can't cry out
when the baby comes, when the knife

slips red on your thumb. Cross the river
at its slimmest when the ice is new.

They will be too cautious to follow.

Carry in one arm a book, in the other a child,
supple legs dangling down your thigh.

They'll think you're much too young to be a mother.

Travel at night
or just before dawn.

Let the darkness wear you.
Let the child dream hot on your neck

as you thread yourself through
an orchard's loose gate seeking windfall.

They have lied to you all along.

You must eat the fruit, girl.
You will need your strength.

You must build a roof from all that's fallen.

Awake at dawn and wanting
      to tell you: I always
   confuse swallow and sparrow.

One is common, brown and white, a householder,
      ground-fed. The other, shy and aerial,
   tail split like my heart. What I meant

to say is one hops the other swoops,
      I can't remember which. When you're gone
   I forget to eat. I forget

when it was I last fed
      the baby, her tucked and hungry
   body curled against me, like a shoot to its seed. No,

like a droplet rippling still water. It's winter now,
      but I remember summer's heavy arms,
   the thick smell of mercy in the air. I remember

when you climbed down in the window well
      to save a sparrow, or a swallow. Or was it me? Yes,
   dead leaves whispering threats at my feet,

the air gone damp and cool. The flying thing,
      her bent and broken departures, blind
   to the sky above her. How quiet

I was, holding her throb and flutter
      in my hands, coaxing her back to flight,
   then climbing up into daylight.

What I meant to say is: The windows
      need washing, the baby sighs
   in her crib, I'm standing here,

late afternoon, looking out
        the front of the house to see
    if I see you. What I meant

to say is, Love, is that you
        coming home or some shadow
    of flight in the failing sun?

AFTER READING THE STORY OF ASSUMPTION CHAPEL IN COLD SPRING, MINNESOTA

The doctor says, Your disease is still ripening.

     Ripening? you ask, and feel your teeth slice late plums

  through to stone. You think of seeds swollen

into fat hearts of summered flesh, then storms

     of locusts shearing bare the fields.

  He says, It may be years. And you watch linens vanish

like dreams, swallowed off clotheslines.

     You see a boy. He is small. He gathers locusts

  like stones that might save him

on a roofless night in the woods. Ten cents a bushel,

     he'll have new boots for winter. The doctor says,

  This is the nature of your disease—long growing

season beset by plague and fire, good years

     and lean. You sigh

  against the hollow cheeks of the farm wives.

Their husbands are building a chapel

     to the Virgin, a hillside plea, small cape

  of prayer. You say, Please, I have built a roof

over my children's heads. It is close to collapse.

     You say it—ripening—, imagine a woman carved

  in stone above a doorway,

rising skyward, her hands

     held out to the locusts at her feet

  as if to say, Yes,

even this.

PERSEPHONE: SINCE SHE KEPT ASKING,

I gave her an answer.
Chose a window with a view

of rough country. Said oak,
said aster. Piled up lies

in her warm brown eyes.
What can she know

of the word *crawlspace*,
of the choiring black

birds that nest
in my hair? Look

out the window, Mom.
The bright moss

is my sash as it tore. The bone-
white road, remnant press

of my spine. The far smoke
is my father's slight

amendment.
Blue mountain,

torn rind
of my heart. And there

in the middle distance, near the house
that kneels, praying, on the hillside—

he is the black horse
barely rendered.

I am the open door.

Fog so thick it drips off the branches
    and swallows every noise. Once
there was a childhood and it looked like this:
    Earth wrapped in a cool blue cloak.
Many years next to each other like books
    on a shelf, and all the gardens opening
their mouths to drink. Summer lasts
    forever. More babies are born,
but they're happy and good sleepers.
    All the trees look young again,
their bark lustrous, deep.
    A sandbox big as a hill. Apples
blush in orchards, late summer.
    Grown-ups linger over coffee,
school bus runs on time. The sun
    is like God—warm, reliable. Steamed
milk and honey before bed.
    World on pause while we wait
for a cloud come down from heaven
    to pass by. All this lasts until
eighth grade, when they tell us
    the sun's a yellow dwarf burning
itself out. Meet my son. He's seven
    and happy. He comes home
from school today through a fog
    that never burned off, that crawled
through cracks in the walls. He lifts,
    he glides, he wheels in a vortex
up the driveway. Comes indoors saying,
    Mom, the sun won't last
forever. Really, Mom. And we're becoming
    extinct. Runs outside again to play.
One feather falls down from his wings.

MOST ACCIDENTS OCCUR AT HOME

Nobody tells you this:
    Every day is a creation story.

You'll make a dome of light over waste and welter
    some of the time, then wake one night

on your side of the bed and remember:
    There weren't many happy endings.

First the ripe fruit. Then the way he turned from her,
    said it was her idea.

Nobody tells you this will happen again
    and again. You'll turn away

from each other, turn back again, wincing
    to touch the bones you vowed to share.

Nobody warns you of the day
    that's bound to come. In this story,

you are tired, you haven't slept
    in years. There are children close

together and meals to get. You
    are in the kitchen getting them.

Your son walks in. You see blood
    on his hands. You know

whose blood it is. You shift
    the baby to the other hip, you breathe

deep, you say, Wash your hands
    and come to the table for dinner.

TWELVE-YEAR QUESTIONS

The air sharp as any spade, but snow
cloaking hillside and roof makes our silence
seem the order of the day.

The same twelve-year questions
stare at us, blank as walls. No answers,
just my hands holding out

a cup of hot coffee as you leave
for work and—chance sacrament—
my knuckle grazes your palm,

cold already
in the doorway. Then
the snowplow's grind and moan.

We're sealed in again.
One sip, you hand the cup back,
grab the shovel,

head down the hill
to dig us out,
second time this morning.

Through frost
and windowpane
I watch your body churn

against another everyday
roadblock. Love, there should be
a word for *to mine the beloved's heart.*

There should be a word
for *go out*
and see what's coming next.

IDIOPATHIC

These rooms never have windows. You're alone
and waiting, still dressed in the endless blue

of their gowns. Outside this room, your whole life
swallows hard. Your husband paces the waiting

room, flinting his fists. You wait like a cold house
waits for a fire to make it warm, wait while the sky

goes down to an early dusk, mending boundaries
and gaps by failing to reveal them. You wait

because you can't unfold, can't rise up,
can't ignore the ladder you climb every day

just to stand on your feet.
When you hear the *tap-tap*

on the door, try to straighten, try to smile, try
to forget the splayed heart flapping in your chest.

Then listen, nod, murmur your thanks, and turn
again toward the ransacked room

of your body.

II

1.

At least there are windows, bright skin
between room and sky. Snow,
but the day is heavy with more
than winter—so many unnamed
or unnameable flaws
of a tender contraption,
hide and bone, we call it the body.
All the kept secrets of blood
and other fugitives prowling
down dim passageways.
Muck and misfire,
scar and bloom. Here in the chairs,
the half-hours creep. Your name
might be next. No, sit tight.
We'll be with you shortly.
Rehearse your story again:
Torn awake
in a loud red room
of pain. Then
the long leaking away
of flesh and years.
                    A door opens
for you. Then the turning
back to see if the one you love
most will follow you down.

2.

Now you are a ladder of bones
and blanks on a lit screen.
Woman of marble
architecture, skinned thing,
and those eyes—bare rooms
where the blue was. Now
you are a frame scraped down
to its parts: true ribs
and false. Ischium, ulna.
All twenty-seven bones
of the hand. The doctor says,
Do you drop things? Yes.
Hopefully not the baby!
Now the baby is all hill
and pearl, curve and petal.
When she's tired, she crawls away
from you, holds up her arms
to the walls. Now you are in a room
where the story ends
the same every time—
everyone empty-handed.

3.

Bedtime, the boys ask, Can we catch it?
Does it ever go away? In the doorway

of your answer is a snuffed-out candle,
a way of saying No that hangs in the air.

You've looked inside the dim house
of your body for years, at the blurred threshold

between mother and creature, where at night
you crouch and try to sleep. You've dreamed it—

ditching your car by the river,
tucking the plates in your purse. Then

a hammer of thought: the children.
There are three now, and you, ebbing.

You've looked long at the river's churn
and hunger, at your two beggar's arms.

You've seen the choice you'd make: Take the one
whose memory goes back longest. Take him

by the scruff of the neck.

4.

This time, another half-lit room, another blue
gown tied loose. They feed you a magic egg.
You think you heard this right. Next,
spread yourself out on a steel table, lie still,
don't fall asleep. A wraith of you flickers,
moonlit, on their screens. They watch
the egg slide down through the deep woods
of your body. Their keyboards click.
Or branches in wind? Incessant. How
can you not think of the bread crumbs
in the boy's pocket, of the crow half-dead
with thirst. How everyone you love keeps
dropping stones into the clear glass
of you. Once upon a time, you believed
little by little does the trick. You believed
the water would rise, limpid and able
to bend light.

5.

You bend as near a stalling fire,
or as a sail flags in day's last wind.
Fold again

toward winter, season of bones
clutching at marrow, season
of weak plans

for broth and woolens, cords
of wood stacked and shifting
against the house.

Gone light, gone landmark.

Comes the cold, its indigo hood.
Blows through
your door, keeps the key.

Holds out its hands
for the last warm thing: hot kite
of flame in your chest.

6.

On the neat branches

    of the decision tree, you are *vague*

        constellation of symptoms. The doctor says,

We may never know. There is enough night sky

    in his words for you to fall

        away in—nebular, Magellanic, aftermath

of chance conflagration and midwife

    to new stars. You've seen the photos, ghost-

        clouds, smoky pillars rising up

like hands, hooked fingers, light-year

    after light-year. The doctor says, Does it hurt

        when I do this? Hands that feed

the edgeless night with small spoons

    of light as they themselves

        are consumed.

7.

Night has finished unraveling. Get up.
The dull knife of the day presses through you.
The thread you strung from your bed
to the kitchen is frayed by years of use.
No god is coming for you, no raft sent out
in the flood. They are still here: the pain,
the slow leak. The children's voices pinging
down the hall. Someone says visitor,
someone says false. A children's game
you almost remember. Someone says safe,
someone says chimney. They laugh,
they clap their hands. They don't
know yet that safe is the shell of an egg.
They're forgetting—on the first page
of every story with a chimney
is a pile of dry limbs
waiting to burn.

8.

In this family
of illness,
the doctor says,
the body
attacks itself. Now

let me take a look
at your hands.

9.

Now you are a warped doorway
into which your children have folded
their bodies. No, leave them
out of this. You are a boat,
stormed and oarless, the anchor line
loosed from its fist of a knot.
How many times can a mother drift
by slow miles and go home again.
Who will unlatch the door
when she returns,
soaked through   corroded   revenant—
all those years beneath
the surface. Listen:
the six light feet of children
who live in a house on shore.
You have taught them
never open the door in the dark,
never talk to strangers.

10.

Studies show
people get used to living
in pain, the doctor says.
He is smiling.
Then all the midnights
well up from the cellar
of you. Half-dreams
of rock and river, the sift
of everything unmoored.
To become a story
of erosion you must first live
in all the hollow cities
of the bones. To become echo
you must learn a forced flight.
A canyon grows deep and marked
through patient years
of dragging away. All
the stacked palimpsests
of lives unearthed—
a feather, a stitch
of spine, some useful tool,
maybe, this chipped edge of stone.
Deeper down, the carvings,
all the colors of birth
or fire. The caves, the caverns.
The intricate, hidden rooms.

III

AT DOCK'S END

The slow ambush
of August
heat, how the hills blur

with it, how the sky
wavers. And
all the sounds

of the world blunted—
hum of unseen
boats, squabbling gulls.

Even the lake's unsure
of its shores if you look
far off, past the man

who stands in the water
holding up his arms
to you, waiting,

about to count. Already
you know every lake
is a remnant,

what's left of glacier's yield
when the world turned
warmer. You know

what rests
on its sepulchral floor—
silt and stone, claw

and husk, lost hooks
and lines. You
have been there before,

playing with your brothers,
a game you call
Drowning.

That benthic roar.
Blue eternally.
This is where you begin—

as breath held
in the moment before.
When the man says,

One two three jump,
everything you do next
is descent.

Even if
he'll catch you,
you're falling.

GRETEL, REPRISE

Who knows now where my brother was. Locked away
for fattening, or gone to the store with our father.

Letter in hand, I walked up grandfather's street
ribboned with trailer homes on the slant, past

the shuffleboard courts. Turned right and counted
three blocks to the letter box. On the way back, turned

too soon into a street that looked the same. The scene tipped
to spill me out. Birdsong vanished. Only blood and the thick

breath of orange blossom swarming my head. My heart a fist. Little girl,
are you lost? A kindly witch in a housecoat, eyes deep

as old tales. Grandfather's name, another language
in my mouth. Through here, she says, pointing

to a narrow place just past her garden wall. Through
the gap, up the half-porch, inside the screen door,

past its slam, home. I flutter on the couch like a moth
whose wing has been held between two fingers,

but gently. My mother pulls something from the oven,
finds me there on the couch crying,

says, Well you're here now.
Come have a bite to eat.

SELF-PORTRAIT AS SOMETHING LIKE A HEART

Barefoot, backdoor, the hum
and clink of a kitchen, breeze

on my back in the storm-blown night—it was never
just a house, that place. One day seeped

into the next. A blue-walled room,
a window, the willow hung with sorrowing

branches, ribbons of shade my inheritance.
There was always one door to slip through

unnoticed, four walls of shelter-
in-place, or the woods closing

its curtain behind me. Listen, there are birds
more often seen than heard, there are words

we fasten to their calls—*Fire fire,*
where where and *Who cooks for you?* Came to a hill

the perfect slant for watching the sky
bruise with storm. Came to an orchard

months beyond fruit. Look, back then my bones
were breastplate, sturdy nest, no need

for the word *relic.* And the plum
tasted something like a heart

should taste—deep, red, sweet
and tart together.

        Tenderly
the slender bow
    of innocence lifts—
  nothing unknown

can be known. The hum
    of not knowing you're lucky
  in life swells like whole rivers

and flows past the window-
    glass, across the field
  where he watches you

as those on a long road gaze
    at a waiting house, knowing
  it's home. So many future hallways

of blood and bone to prowl
    down, your cheeks
  so deliciously pale.

In one legend, the wolf fears
    the sound of bow on string.
  In another,

the rich saw and thrum
    resemble his dreams—a mother
  who used to sing

"Clementine," that season of milk
    and denning. That you dream,
  too, means nothing

to him, that you sleep curled
    and fetal in your bed.
  If it were night

and he were hungry, he'd thrust
        his muzzle starward
    and howl the pain into your

limbs. But it's morning. You're reaching
        for pages, shuffling
    for just the right song—clean

opening note. Something
        andante, no rush. He paws
    at the first shoots now breaking

through. His eyes prefer a thicket
        for framing, but the window
    will do. And the lure

of music. And your unearned body
        still so supple,
    so blank.

GIRL WITH BOOK AND ANGEL

Everyone watches a girl unfold
into woman, and I hid
in the shade

of my thorn-dark hair
when my father's friends looked at me
too long. In the cool rooms

of summer days and books when Mother
was tired, wanting help. But the angel
I never expected. So coarse, reckless wings,

no manners at all. Came in wild
while I read on the porch,
looked long at me.

I knew enough to hold
my hands like blades, look him in the eye,
grant him his words all full of holes—

Behold   your
      womb
will   overshadow you.

Some girls learn to fight, to flee.
As for me, once released,
I hopped on my bike and rode down the street

to see my cousin,
older than me, but also stained
fresh with God.

That night I learned to see love in a trigger finger—
Dixie coming to finish the job, Dick's horse having slipped
the pasture, having met with a luckworn Ford.
Love in the blessed moan of the six o'clock whistle
calling men in from the fields for supper. Love even
in the way the Baptist preacher stepped across his doorway
to keep me from his house. Love in his voice, 2 Corinthians,
Be ye not yoked with unbelievers. I wanted to say, I do believe.
In the waving quilt of fields shook out and settled here
on Earth. And every so often a limping barn,
a slumped house. And every so often a tidy one. I believe
in the way the right-angled roads always ended
at the speck of town on the map—its righteous blocks
and steeples, its tired lake fringed with reeds, the dump
of sand we called the beach. In the water tower, wooden
and dark against a lingering pastel dusk. All summer
with Jane on her parents' porch. Diet Cherry 7 Up
and who kissed who for how long where—against
Emmons' barn, out Derby Road, maybe in the meadow
called Tall Tall Grass. I believe in the night
Tracey died, the night Kelley died, the shoe thrown
from a car on the front page and my mother turning
the paper face down on the table. In the songs we sang
after, *How great Thou.* I believe in all those winter miles
of gym floor Wesley swept at half-time. In the quick flip
of the Bic he pulled from his pocket to light the altar
candles on his wedding day. I believe in my brother
bent and weeping in Jane's hair the day Ty
swallowed his death with a sip of water. I believe
in wood smoke, windbreak, a gravel road strolling along
to a place where the next field is the memory of a field
of stars in the dwindling light. We've tried
to make them ours, pressed our stories on the night's
specked canvas. The northern bear, the hunter, the woman
who talked too much of her own allure. Shape
of all questions—who, what, when (where did Lisa hide
her baby all that time?). Odd-angled beauty, night-strung,

always somewhat upside down. We never knew her name,
would not have known how to say it. I believe
in the way she leans and circles the pole forever, in her
hunched shoulders, stained hand. Erratic. Variable.
Given to occasional outbursts in brightness.

EPITHALAMIUM WITH TRAIL OF ASHES

with lines from "The Robber Bridegroom"

When the right kind of man came along, I woke
in a room stacked with waiting plates, my very own spoons.

The day broke warm on the outskirts of winter. I bathed,
dressed early, cinched my grandmother's gold on my neck.

Pictures, my brothers laughing. Someone said, You should eat.
Someone said, I will make you a trail of ashes. *Me*?

Later he'd say he went for breakfast, felt sick, got caught
on the far side of town by the train. The quiet song

of the front door hinge caused my heart to break.
Bare-armed, I waited, one last borrowed room

bundled with flowers and chairs. The organ began,
optimistic. Later I'd say, Let me tell you a dream I had:

the naïve light of morning, my dad's warm arm,
that red aisle, tether and bridge. A line of fine men

on the altar, him first and hiding a smile. Later
we'd say something showed us the way

in the moonlight, that we walked all night.
The wind had scattered the ashes.

A house standing all by itself. I wandered
from one room to the next.

And here is the finger with the ring still on it.

THE OBJECTS OF FAITH

Window

To begin as sand and salt

To crush, mix, melt in fire

To go suddenly sheer, spill out
over molten metal, cool slowly

To be cut to size

To hang in someone's house,
their kitchen

To flare at sunset, spill
lamplight into darkness, tremble
against storm wind

To wear a veil of frost in winter,
to feel warm breath on your back

To hold in place
one piece of the world—moon
in the oak's arms, brushstroke

of road unspooling, inked
silhouette

of one who stands waiting

Berry

To grow low, wet, evergreen

To bloom pink
with arms thrown back

To set pale fruit,
to deepen, flame

To spill out over wide water
when ripe

To shine blood-bright in someone's hands,
their kitchen

To meld with their sugar

To boil, burst, liquefy

To settle jewel-deep
into another's shape

To be that ache
in someone's mouth

Basket

To begin slender
in a slow river, wading

To curtain the seam
where water skims land

To come loose from your roots,
be gathered, carried
you know not where

To relinquish your long greening,
go hollow, fade

To revive in water, to soften

To sway in someone's hands,
their kitchen

To be woven, half-done, half-
done for months, for seasons

To pick up again, tender weave,
meet yourself coming round

To be vessel, full
then empty, then full again

To bear that weight

To be bridged with a place
for holding

NOVEMBERING

How can I explain? I feel him
remembering me. His songs of lost

seasons lace through
my ribs, and in my veins

dreams of that first winter
thaw and flow. Even as I gather

late apples, dry leaves
stutter in the wind like his regrets—

the thieving, the blindfold,
the groundward ride.

Who would believe
that by the time of rain

and runoff, he'd become almost tender,
wading my homesick waters, culling smooth stones

to stack on our table, pulling out
my chair. Mom, he built a house for me

and the rooms, though dark,
are budding. The windows gleam like scars

of my own skin. Mom, it's years now
and my hand knows the curve

of his back, my bones give way
to the opening door

of his voice saying *winter.*
These waning days

are the pitch of his roof gathering in
my weak protests, becoming wind

and wingspan
of the only life I know.

The wild night flight—second to the right,
straight on till morning—through a spangled sky
flecked with fairies who you still thought were all good.

Then the first look at the island, unknown and yet
known. Neverland. Your heart in your throat, for soon
there would be campfires and mermaids and little lost boys.

Even the kiss—or was it a button?—that saved
your life when the arrow struck and the rust
of blood in your mouth didn't alert you.

And then their grief and whispers,
their joy at the mere fluttering of your hand,
and the house they built up all around you.

This was before you woke from your faint
and remembered: You were only a girl,
with no experience.

Except this time you did grow up, and now
you must decide: Will you be a lady or a bird or a witch?
Look: The sky grows grim, snow is falling.

And listen: All the lost boys are waiting outside,
shivering. Asking, Where is our dinner?
Tapping on the windows, calling, Wake up, wake up—

IV

FIRST HOUSE

Some women marry houses.
It's another kind of skin . . . —Anne Sexton

1.

So many whites—
siding, shades, baseboards. The walls,
the clock's wide face, bleached
sheets thinning in their beds. Shells
of eggs, the patient milk, clothesline
strung like a weak pact
between porch and fence. Somewhere
a dress, a veil folded
away in a box. Sometimes
the moon, when you remember
the moon, a scuffed stone past the afternoon
window. Towels, bread, the winter
spinning its wool—drift
and wind chill, ice, an apron
of snow on the roof. The children,
their faces lined up pale and hungry. Each day
more faded than the last. Even the trees
wear shrouds, want out, hold on
to a last leaf or two against wind
and whiteout—proof
of other seasons.

2.

Here is the mirror
where your eyes drag over
the bleak walls
of your body, the lock
of pain on your wasting
frame, shelf of cheekbone,
staircase of rib rib
numberless rib, the eaves
of each hipbone,
colding.

Here are the elbowed stairs
you gave up on. Here is the boy—
sapling, swing—whose name
you called, and the place he found
the crumpled heap
of you, said, Scoot down, Mom, I'll help.
And you can sleep on the couch tonight.

Here is the attic bedroom
where years ago you stowed
the cracked cup
of hope beneath the bed
for safekeeping. Where the bed
is a far meadow under snow,
undisturbed.

3.

House of skeleton
key, cold spot, creak
and draft. Stunted
garden, falling fence.

What is a storm
but too much happening at once?

Already the boys know
to hunch at the register
for warmth.

4.

In this house, every day is a riddle.
Pull the wrong half-limp from the drawer
and it all falls down.

Step
on a crack
and you break.

In the backyard, the boys are trying
to build a fort with snow
that's too cold to pack,
that falls in piles
of tiny shards
at their feet.

The baby's islanded
on her blanket in the corner.
When you call her name,
she doesn't look your way.

Your husband comes through the door each night
trailing a slice of winter.

5.

At some point, the cold runs out
of options. The crocus
shoves its dumb face
through wasting scraps of snow.

Next, slender blades
of grass, small nubs
of green in the river birch.

Screen doors unlatching
all along the street.

They say the river crests tonight at midnight.

6.

Do you see that? The trees
pull on their long sleeves
of green. The lilacs burst
open in May
as if they don't know
what's happened
on the other side
of the window they fill.

7.

When the radio screeches
its storm warning, fill the bathtub,
grab the kids, head for the lowest place.

You remember buying this house,
its long list of faults, the water line
on the basement wall.

You remember thinking, here
is where my life will happen. And it did—
shelves and drawers

built under the stairs, low hum
of fluorescent bulbs, the rows
of nails and screws glinting in their jars.

8.

Lived to wake
one day in a room
beyond winter. Lived

to feel sap rise
in your veins, the pelt
of new flesh round

all your corners,
late fruit.

Sold the house.

Left the birdhouse come July.
There were nestlings.

9.

Mary says the trees have all come down,
the whole street's skeletal. Even from the edge
of the map you feel the pull of the house
mourning its thick flank of shade. The roof
won't wait for you, is already longing for collapse—
tide or monument, the scattering stars.
And the street picked clean, the unforgiving sun.
And the house bleached and white,
worn smooth by years and the turn
of the Earth—relic, shell,
small stone on a slipping shore.

V

VERNAL

Watch at your window the light
          break in the bare hands
     of trees. Let it bring what passes for warmth.

First morning in years
          that feels gradual—the pain
     no longer a wall

you slam into upon waking.
          Instead, an old coat,
     scuffed, persistent.

Some meadow somewhere quivers
          under snow.
     It may be inside you. It may

be the stuck hinge
          of your body loosening
     at last. Watch the sky—

how it takes on a pale gold wash,
          almost sallow. Watch
     a shawl of long-held snow slide free

of the neighbor's roof
          into your shade garden,
     where nothing thrives exactly,

where each May the indigo bunting
          calls out its warning,
     Fire, fire.

Now do something
          you haven't rehearsed,
     spool and spindle,

the cloth you've woven
         for years—
      lay it down.

ON A DRIVE THROUGH THE COUNTRY MY DAUGHTER ASKS, MOM, WHAT IS THAT OUT THERE, ALL THOSE TREES AND NO HOUSES?

And I want to show her a mirror, speak
        of apples and huntsmen. I want to warn her:
    Remember the boy, his white dove, the vanished
breadcrumbs. Remember Grandmother, her shifting
        jawline, sharpening ears. She asks, Where
    are the neighborhoods, where are the stores?
Should I tell her? That whole towns mistake
        nearness for safety, and the backyard fence
    falls in every storm as she sleeps. In the red house
down the street, the mother is sick.
        In the white house with green trim.
    There are only so many pots of soup you can take
next door, and then what. She asks, Where
        are all the streets, where are the streetlamps?
    And the front porch cleaves from the house
a little more in each cold snap. And the one
        I took for a prince is late for dinner
    most nights. Is it time to pull out
the book I have stashed in my drawer?
        The diagrams, the labeled parts, the man
    and the woman. The house they've built
together, stacking year on year. She asks,
        Does the school bus come here, does the mail?
    Yes, and still at the edge of the garden,
roses bramble toward wild and the ash
        sows its seedlings like thirst. And the man,
    the woman—every spring they pull, they hack,
they try to beat it all back.

PERSEPHONE, MIDSUMMER

I no longer know how I came to be here.
She claimed me? He returned me?

A cleaving, more light
than I'm used to now, then everyone pretending

I've never been anywhere else,
here at the sink, tasting summer

in my mother's kitchen, washing plates
until their painted edges fade.

But I've taken on the green
of his river. I'm listening

for the whine of his dog
wanting my hand on its warm belly,

for the long hall
of his walk coming up from behind.

He says there are children now,
open-mouthed and spindling

toward light. A tree we planted
that fruits in red. Debts

that sound somehow familiar.
A deal I struck once—

the way I left off tending, hoping
growing things would know to dig

for what they needed
deeper, down.

FLARE

Call it a drum or a slamming
door's reverberation. Hair spread
on a pillow in red's not it. Try net
of hot wires lit from within,
a tensing coil, the failing coals
of a just-banked fire, a tree
branching rough through the bones.
Inside, a howling roams
all my hallways, a gale
of footsteps builds in my limbs.
Call it unwalled again, estuary
bleeding, place of surge and husks
left behind. The meat's
all-day simmer, a bed never made,
the rains swamping the cellar
for months. The saints all descend
on my barren kitchen, drop stones
in the draining jar of my days.
I dull, I trickle long trails—
pills and needles, jeweled vials,
a river of blood coaxed out
of my veins. Call it thrum
and spinning, rim-bent, warped.
Make it of huddle and pulse,
hunch and vise-grip, a roof
pressing up on a slow-moving storm.
Tell me how to dream a fist
unfurling, the crawl of pain
to some other shore. Tell me
this is worth something—that I'll burn
a blacker trail along the earth.

ELEGY

You're still waiting for charms against night
and lostness. I know the song of the wood thrush,

stitch of the clock. I know latchkey and outskirts
are just different ways of going home. Willow, milkweed,

the sewer grate where the wasps rose up
like fevered prayers. The pages of books

to shelter between. I've been remembering you
as I sing my flatland girl to sleep—*ee-oh-lay*

ee-oh-lay—just so she'll know there were songs. I lie.
I say the flood was only a dream, the wild beast

prowls only in the hills. Her cheek
is a wing on my passerine heart. My heart,

its fondness for perch and undergrowth, scatter
of last year's leaves. I won't speak

of Orion, how holes in his belt outshine
our sun, or his shoulder waiting to spill

its terrible light in our daytime sky.
And if the house should shake

with the gait of a transient earth,
if drought should snag

in the backs of our throats
for good, at least she'll have known

my voice in the wandering
moment of sleep falling down. Girl I was,

you keep asking the way
fledglings beg at an empty nest. Go back

to your shirtless, half-boy, August afternoons.
Go to your footpath, your hill of shade.

And if your feet lose their way, watch out
for spindle and kiss, the time the match burned

down to your hand. And if you look to me
for assurances from a future map,

all I can say is I haven't yet told you all I know
of winter, the bruise

of late fruit, and all these books still split
open in my hands.

LOVE POEM FOR LUPUS

with lines from "Little Red Riding Hood"

There's always a house alone in the wood,
three oaks to mark the place, a hazel hedge.
The roof is a slanted pledge.

I've worn the pelt of forest shade.
I've worn my little hood of red.
The path is aching with thaw.

When I find the house alone in the wood,
I'm always a tender young thing.
Grandmother's dead six years.

There is sorrow.
Birds in winter plume.
Salt for the deer to nose.

There are children
with voices bright as coins.
The tall, bent steps. The wolf

raised the latch and the door swung wide
open years ago now. There may be a fire
with hands for flames. There may be a witch,

an oven stoked. Surely a bed turned down
for me. A rug at the hearth where the wolf
sleeps. The *tick-tick-tick* of his heart.

I know how to dread him—
dread like a trip wire, dread like thirst.
I've ungloved my hands,

eaten the cakes, drunk the wine.
The huntsman is otherwise occupied.
Here is the only place. I wake

every day in this story, call in the children, open wide
this breakable body, this hard-won room, this house
of luck and bone that made us.

TRANSVERSE

—Syn. *crosswise, bent, intersecting; see* oblique

The new house has solid oak doors,
a woodstove, and moths.

And all our favorite, tattered fights
which we unpack from the last-on-first-off box

with the coffeepot and the phone, some paper plates,
some matches. A cloud of wings

in every corner and closet. I ignore them, hoping
they'll go once we crowd the house

with all our books and pans and breath and the general hum
of living. But box after box they stay,

dusty, persistent. They haunt
cupboards, lampshades, drapes. They dig

holes in our blankets for nests, fly
toward the one light we leave burning in the kitchen

in the night, mistake it
for something celestial.

You say, They're small, they don't eat much.
You say, What did you expect—we live in the woods.

And I have to agree with you there, about living deep
and with deadfall, far

from the village. About nesting wherever
it's warm and flying toward whatever

light's left
          burning.

SELF-PORTRAIT AS A BACKWARD GLANCE

There are roads that lead out
past landmarks. It's true
there was a veil once, that somehow

it lifted. It's true that I vowed
I would. All the days of my life
went on like before—porch light,

moth, a simmering on the back
of the stove. It's true that next the bowl
of my body was hearth for kindling

bone, assembling
limbs. That the skies tore,
whole cities fell, a bridge

forgot the way home. It's true
that wars bloomed on the skin
of the Earth and the kitchen

floor had a cold spot.
The root cellar filled
with old paint, yes, all the trees

in the yard too tall for climbing.
There is a story of a woman who looked
back—bent roof, ash

in the grate, the clatter
in the ribcage is called the heart.
There is a story of another woman, a cry

that scaled her throat and flew off
on dark wings. It's true
that next she turned

pale and mineral, rooted
and tasting of her own skin
and tears. It's true

that she's still standing.

POEM THAT BEGINS ON A STAIRCASE

Night's kinship behind me now,
    the bed's dream-shaken,
  desolate sheets.

Out the window, a blithe blue sky
    I traded for all those gales.
  And morning rising up the stairs

like smoke from a low fire—
    news of other rooms
  and longitudes,

Police Swarm Hostage Sites Killing Gunmen.
    Woman Killed by Truck
  Carrying Bees. Mom, did you know

we're out of milk again. The kitchen now—
    the watched pot,
  the hand that feeds. The children

are older, have unraveled
    from my side. And my love
  always brittle anyway, breaking

where it should bear
    weight. Still,
  every morning I startle

at their flight,
    their bright, unworried departures.
  Door to the jagged world

open wide, and their bodies
    clinking through it
  like the day's loose change.

Shapes of your life climbing up out of night—
a doorway, a stack of books. And all the gaps

that dreams leave (how finally the bird
had nested, how somehow you were the bird).

A side yard where peaches redden
like girls becoming women, a key
that opens a door to a house where you live.

Where the floorboards hold.
Where the roof has not flown off and left you,
and water falls from faucets every time you turn them on.

You hardly know what to do with these riches.

See yourself as a softness turning
with the Earth. See the children in their beds
breathing, metronomic.

Your parents are alive.
Your husband was not on the lost plane.
It will rain all day next Wednesday.

The day has brought itself to you like an offering,
has stretched its muslin light across the stars.

The stars are still there, waiting.
Night will come again, a mercy.

The infection went away, the jasmine's blooming,
yesterday, Mary called.
Her voice opened doors all through you.

It is the season of stone fruit, of prodigal flesh
come home, whose warmth unfolds down the length
of a tender trap—the body you've learned

to live in. Its subtle bars, a window scuffed
with years and small storms.

The way it lets the light in, even so.

ADMISSION

Every year I tried to stop the barely felt tilting—
Earth turning its shoulders
from the sun. I watched

the afternoon shadows lean
toward the seam of land
and sky, while she sang

and skipped, rode her bike
around the block, forgot
her sun hat one last time.

She didn't know the stories I knew—
Andromeda and the minor-key
clank of her chains,

the way we laughed at Cassandra's
raw tales, then wept
as they came true.

Every year I wanted to tell her
why—the season
of cold and blind

untangling nights, the gnarled
and patient hands of winter
laying out bowls

on a blank table. The way
she'd tinge gray, unstrung
by hunger and waiting. That I, too, once

saw that fruit lit with the promise
of flesh and blood,
and ate.

Notes

The epigraph for the collection is Emily Dickinson's poem 135 from *The Complete Poems of Emily Dickinson*, edited by Thomas H. Johnson (New York: Little, Brown, and Company, 1961).

"After Reading the Story of Assumption Chapel in Cold Spring, Minnesota": Assumption Chapel was built in the late 1870s in petition to the Blessed Virgin Mary for relief from a cycle of Rocky Mountain locust infestations that ruined the wheat harvests of 1873–77.

"Persephone: Since she kept asking,": The landscape described in this poem was inspired by the painting *View of the Campagna*, 1832, by Friedrich Wasmann; oil on paper mounted on cardboard, Hamburger Kunsthalle.

"Picture of the Sun": The title is from Emily Dickinson's poem 188 from *The Complete Poems of Emily Dickinson*, edited by Johnson.

"How to Lure the Wolf": The title is a chapter heading from M. F. K. Fisher's book *How to Cook a Wolf* (New York: North Point Press, 1988).

"Girl with Book and Angel": This poem was inspired by the work of Mary Szybist in her collection *Incarnadine* (Minneapolis: Graywolf Press, 2013). The sixth stanza is an erasure of Luke 1:30–35 from *The Catholic Study Bible: New American Version*, edited by Donald Senior (New York: Oxford University Press, 1990).

"Portrait of Hometown as Constellation": The last sentence of the poem is borrowed directly from the description of the constellation Cassiopeia in *Star Tales*, by Ian Ridpath (New York: Universe Press, 1988).

"Epithalamium with Trail of Ashes": This poem borrows from two versions of the fairy tale "The Robber Bridegroom": one from *The Grimm Reader: The Classic Tales of the Brothers Grimm*, translated and edited by Maria Tartar (New York: W. W. Norton and Company, 2010), and the other from D. L. Ashliman's translation of the story told by Jacob and Wilhelm Grimm, accessed January 19, 2019, https://www.pitt.edu/~dash/grimm040.html.

"The Objects of Faith": The title is a line from Jorie Graham's poem "The Way Things Work," from her collection *Hybrids of Plants and of Ghosts* (Princeton, NJ: Princeton University Press, 1980). The three object poems were inspired by Connie Wanek's poem "Pumpkin," from her collection *On Speaking Terms* (Port Townsend, WA: Copper Canyon Press, 1986).

"First House": The epigraph is from Anne Sexton's poem "Housewife," from her collection *All My Pretty Ones*, in *The Complete Poems* (New York: Houghton Mifflin Company, 1999).

"Love Poem for Lupus": Some lines and phrases in this poem were suggested by two versions of the Little Red Riding Hood tale: "Little Red Riding Hood," *Fairy Tales from the Brothers Grimm: A New English Version*, edited by Philip Pullman (New York: Penguin, 2012); and "Little Red Riding Hood," *The Grimm Reader: The Classic Tales of the Brothers Grimm*, translated and edited by Maria Tartar (New York: W. W. Norton and Company, 2010). The phrase "The wolf raised the latch and the door swung wide open" is a direct quote from the Tartar version, although in the poem I have left out a comma between "latch" and "and."

"Transverse": The epigraph is from the entry for *transverse* in *Webster's New World Roget's A–Z Thesaurus*, edited by Charlton Laird (Cleveland: Wiley Publishing, Inc., 1999).

"The Day Has Brought You Everything You Need": The title is a line from Joanna Klink's poem "Vireo," from her collection *Circadian* (New York: Penguin, 2007).

Acknowledgments

Grateful acknowledgement is made to the editors and staff of these publications, in which the following poems first appeared, sometimes in different forms and under different titles:

Bellingham Review: "Onset"

Beloit Poetry Journal: "Demeter, Searching," "Persephone, Midsummer"

Blackbird: "Elegy," "Poem That Begins on a Staircase"

Calyx: "Girl with House and Lost Boys"

Cave Wall: "Survival Guide for the Girl Trying to Avoid Capture," "Picture of the Sun"

Crab Creek Review: "Revision and Aubade"

Copper Nickel: "Portrait of Hometown as Constellation"

Country Dog Review: "Basket" and "Window" from "The Objects of Faith"

The Georgia Review: "Idiopathic," "How to Lure the Wolf," "Flare" as "Love Songs for Lupus"

Heron Tree: "Transverse"

The Massachusetts Review: "Gretel, Reprise"

Memorious: "Love Poem for Lupus," "At Dock's End"

Mid-American Review: "Girl with Book and Angel"

The Missouri Review: "After Reading the Story of Assumption Chapel in Cold Spring, Minnesota"

New England Review: "Self-Portrait as the River Floods," "Self-Portrait as Something Like a Heart"

North American Review: "Most Accidents Occur at Home"

On The Seawall: "The Day Has Brought You Everything You Need"

saltfront: "On a Drive through the Country, My Daughter Asks, Mom, What Is That Out There, All Those Trees and No Houses?"

San Pedro River Review: "Twelve-Year Questions"

Thrush Poetry Journal: "Berry" from "The Objects of Faith," "Persephone: Since she kept asking," "Novembering"

Tinderbox Poetry Journal: "Epithalamium with Trail of Ashes"

"Love Poem for Lupus" also appeared at *Verse Daily*.

"Girl with House and Lost Boys" is for Sarah Kirkwood; "Portrait of Hometown as Constellation" is for Jane Wyckoff-Kingshott.

Although *Hinge* is my second published collection, it's the first one I wrote. Deep gratitude to mentors, friends, and fellow poets who helped me sustain my belief in this book despite its long road to publication. Special thanks to Jennifer Richter, the first to believe. Thank you to Rick Barot for crucial help shaping the manuscript and to Vermont Studio Center for time and space to bring it into its final form. To Jon Tribble, of blessed memory, and Allison Joseph, thank you for your years-long faith in my work; thank you for saying *yes* when the time was ripe. To everyone at the Crab Orchard Series in Poetry and Southern Illinois University Press, thank you for bringing this book into the world with such care. Finally, never-ending thanks to my parents, my extended family, and my friends and neighbors in Saint Paul, Minnesota, who carried my children and me through the years these poems are born of.

Other Books in the Crab Orchard Series in Poetry